A

ANIMAL SHAPES

BRIAN WILDSMITH

Oxford University Press

OXFORD NEW YORK TORONTO MELBOURNE

Lion

Giant Panda

Zebra

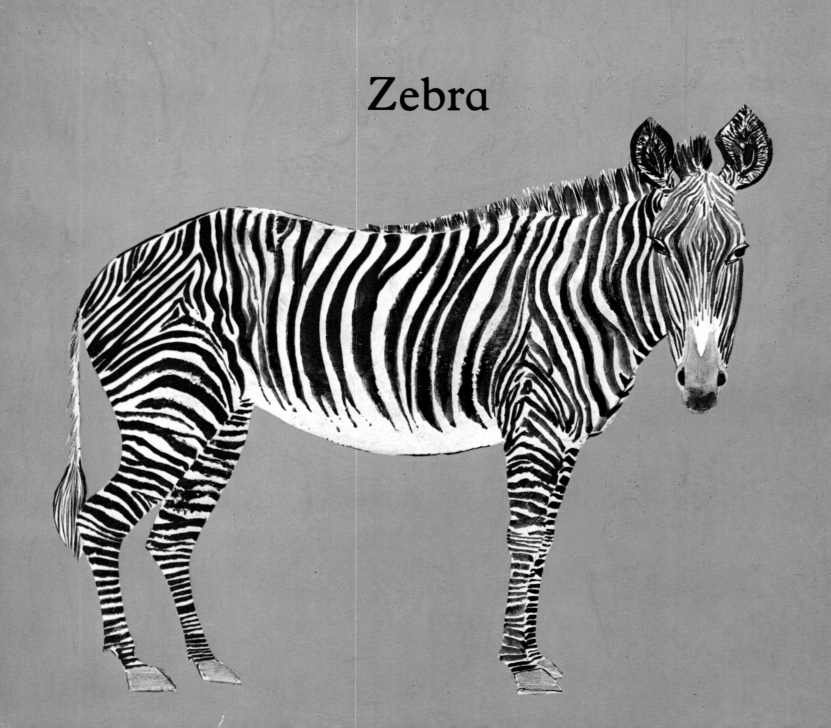

Squirrel

Coati

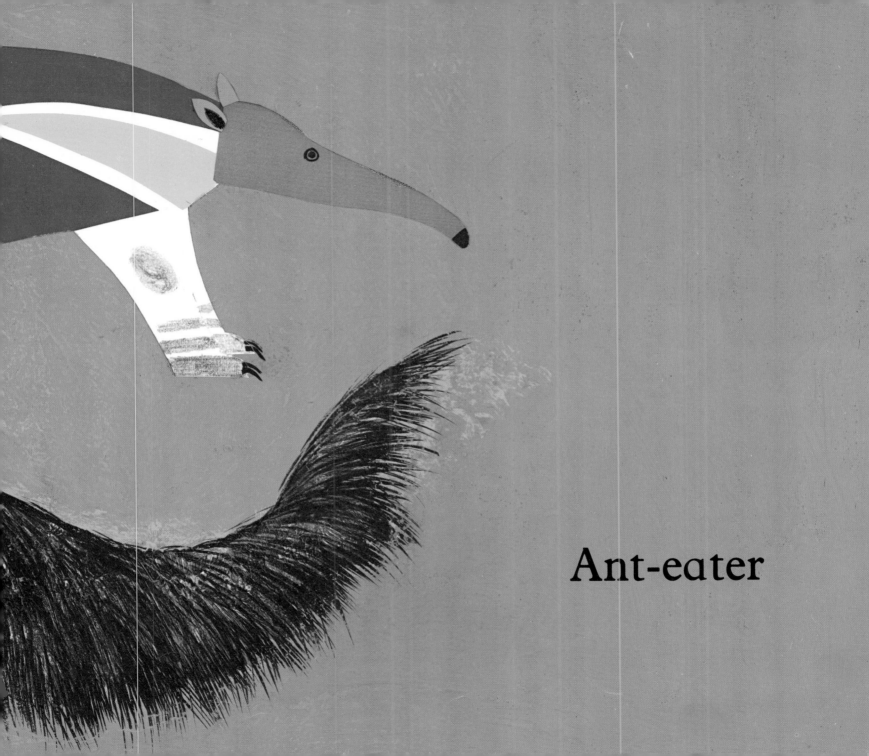

Ant-eater

Elephant

Goat

Rhinoceros

Jaguar

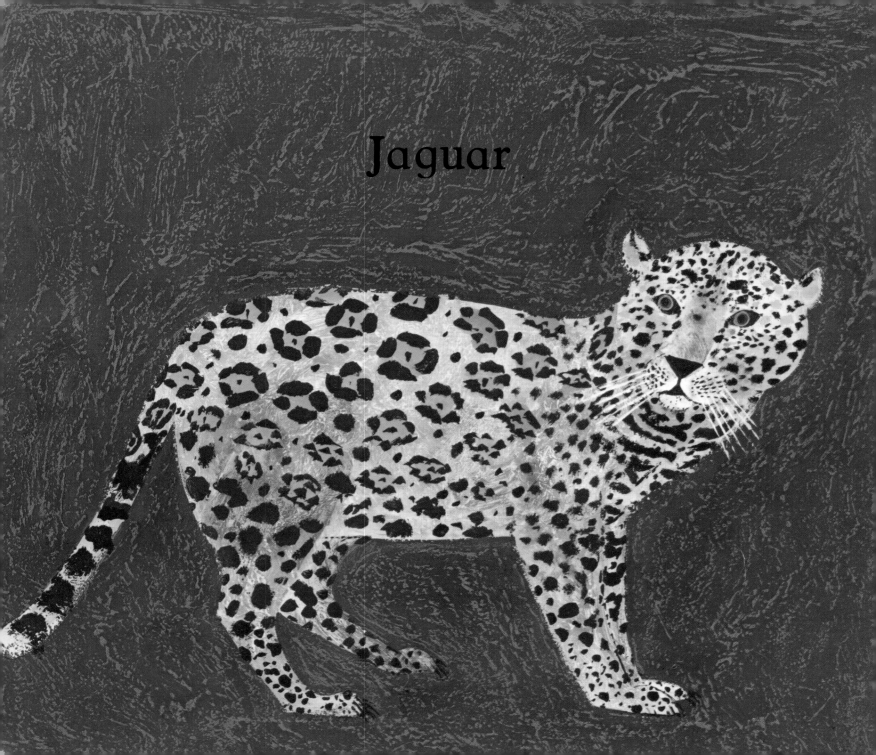

Gnu

Platypus

Oxford University Press, Walton Street, Oxford OX2 6DP
Oxford is a trade mark of Oxford University Press
© Brian Wildsmith 1980
First published 1980   Reprinted 1983, 1990
First published in paperback 1991   ISBN 0 19 279733 6 (hardback)   ISBN 0 19 272174 7 (paperback)
Printed in Hong Kong